Local Voices
An Evening of Poetry

April 18, 2025

DANCING CROWS
PRESS

All rights reserved. No part of this book may be used or reproduced in any manner whatsoever without written permission except in the case of brief quotations embodied in critical articles and reviews.

ISBN 13: 978-1-951543-44-0

Copyright 2025 © Carrollton Writers Guild

Cover design by Kathy Abney

Printed in the United States of America

Dedication

Celebrating the memory of

Eleanor Wolfe Hoomes

A Talented Poet

A Singular Woman

A Pillar of the Art Community

A Mentor

But most of all

A Friend

Poems written in loving memory of Eleanor Wolfe Hoomes

Title	Author	Page
Gone	Robert Covel	1
Lovely Face	Alan Caldwell	2
On Being Human	Cecilia Lee	3
Ode to a Poet	Anne Halliwell	4
For Eleanor	Jessica Munn	5
To My Beautiful Friend	Carol Abney	6

Poetry performed by members of the Carrollton Writers Guild Just Poetry Group

Title	Author	Page
First Day	Richard Allen Anderson	8
Sally's Birthday Party		9
School Lunch		10
Ponderings	Cecilia Lee	12
Traveling Light		13
Carey's Sunday Morning Nap		14
Love Overflowing		15
Come In		15
Connection	Jessica Munn	17
Graham		18
A Poem's Power	Cliff Perkins	20
Wolf	Dave Rozek	22
Lazy Kat Blu		23
My Baby's Gone Blu		24
Eagle		25
That Kind of Friend	Gil Royal	26
Beside the Shore		27
Your Inviting Eyes		28
Cherish is the Word		29
Swan Song	Robert C. Covel	31

Impermanence		32
Knowing Where Your Shoes Are		33
Sacred Places In and Out	Anne Halliwell	35
The New Year		36
Why I Go to Waffle House		37
Butterfly	Marc LaFountain	39
i earth air		40
plants and i		41
Falling Leaves		43
Titanium	Alan Caldwell	46
Variety		48
Almon Street	Carol Abney	52
The Gift		54
Age is Just a Number		56

Poems written in loving memory of Eleanor Wolfe Hoomes

Gone (For Eleanor)

In the still chill
Of a late January pre-dawn,
A terse email announcement:
A vital Presence

Now an absence.
The garden waits for the gardener.
The book of poems awaits the poet's hand.

We look at one another
Askance
Confused, in silence
At the empty chair.

The last poem of a book about life and love
Now written.
Stay on the Path,
Just around the bend, the beloved companion

Awaits,
Just turn the page.

The still unwritten sonnet
(The poet uncomposed)
Finds the final hopeful couplet:
From winter's dark and chill repose
Come springtime's warmth and brilliant rose.

Robert C. Covel

Lovely Face (For Eleanor)

when darkness veils a
lovely face
and marbled stone hallows
modest soil
when none but lines and
stanzas tell
and even rhymes like
surgeons fail
when chairs at friendly tables
sit empty
and every friendly face
shows sorrow
when hope is built on
modest sand
and only few hear
angel bands
we press our helpless palms
and wait
when darkness veils a
lovely face
good bye

Alan Caldwell

On Being Human (Missing Eleanor)

Overcast and foggy
Cloudy and dark
Mourning a friend
Searching for guiding lights.

Our journey, a collection of moments,
Ups and downs, intricacies, surprises, yearnings.
Death.
Searching for sources of courage and strength.

I say to myself:
All shall be well, clouds will pass,
Challenges will untangle,
Opportunities will unfold.

Yet, death is forever
I step out my door, focused,
Appreciated her life journey
Abundance, generosity,
Talents, joy.
Above all: a dear friend
I cherish her memory.

Cecilia Lee

Ode to a Poet

We hate to have a poet die
There are not enough of us
To see the world with clarity

Is unusual
To see life from many angles
Is a gift most don't have
And we value them
We don't want to let go of them

We remember their great poetry
And their voice
They, in a way, helped us write our own poetry
Helping us form our own ideas and poems

We send you love
You probably have already
Formed a poetry group in Heaven
The angels are happily writing away

I just want to say
You taught us a lot
Determination and being brave
Were just a part of your story

We miss you
We hope you are happy
Send us some inspiration if you have time
Say hi… to Jesus for us

Anne Halliwell

For Eleanor

"Here." She says with commanding authority
"They're signed. Read them."
She thrusts a stack of books into my hands
I want to adequately convey my gratitude
Tell her I've already read them all
Rave that she's practically a celebrity to me
Express how I wish I had been the one
To describe Ingrid Bergman's voice
As honey and sand
Explain how I felt tears well up
When she wrote of her mother
Wandering through her own paintings
"On a pilgrimage to The Land of Advancing Silence"
I want to tell her how I've sprawled
Beneath a great oak tree
My cat purring and rubbing
The corners of his mouth
On my copy of Green Thumbs
I think of telling her
Her writing has made me feel
Powerful
Feminine
Awestruck
But instead I just say "Thanks, Eleanor."

Jessica Munn

To My Beautiful Friend, Eleanor Wolfe Hoomes

Making our lives brighter
In a million brilliant and beautiful ways,
A star shining, una hermosa estrella,
Such beauty of purpose and light,

Eleanor was an editor, leader, mentor, hostess,
Organizer, activator, and most importantly,
A friend.

What is love?
Sages discuss the term,
Songwriters attempt to amplify love's meaning,
But
Eleanor *lived* the word love.

Her actions, her beauty and strength,
Exemplified love of community,
All others,
And the arts.
We miss Eleanor deeply,
But we are never truly without her.
Eleanor's influence shines brightly in each of us.
We remember her encouraging words,
A guide onward, always forward,
Even now.

Beautiful friend, brilliant writer, shining star,
Eleanor Wolfe Hoomes.

Carol Abney

Local Voices: An Evening of Poetry

Poetry performed by members of the Carrollton Writers Guild

Just Poetry Group

Richard Allen Anderson

First Day

Why can't I stay here with you,
Just like I always do?
Well, you will like it
You will learn new things.
I like it when you read to me
I already know my ABCs.
You will have a real teacher.
You will meet lots of kids.
Okay, Mom. I'll give it a try
But can you please, please stay nearby?
You'll love Mrs. Armstrong,
She's really pretty and good.
But, Mom you're the most pretty
In this whole big city.

The school building stood tall and gray
With double doors and stairways inside.
I watched and wondered as Mom walked away,
Should I follow the others or should I hide?
We sat looking up at our surrogate mom
While she read to us or we sang
Until my heart became more calm
And much later that day the school bell rang.

Mom hugged me and kissed me
When I ran in the door.
Here's a cookie. Tell me how was your day?
We painted with fingers!
We napped on the floor!
I could tell she was happy.
I could tell she was sad.
It hurts, Mom, don't hug me so tight.
Okay, my big boy, now go tell your dad.

Sally's Birthday Party

What I remember most about Sally Naschef
Is not her dense waist, dark complexion, and thick black hair
(Although, I remember all that too)
Is how she drew up big Edward Warner,
The biggest boy in our class,
To dance with her
At her first teen-age birthday party.

In the dim shadows of the basement rec room
No ray of light can pass between their
Close -pressed stance as they sway and dance
To swing music of the 40s
From the stack of 78s on Sally's brand new
Birthday present record player.

I wonder if my young classmates,
Wiilliam Keller, Shirley Kittleson, and Audry Schmidler,
Now gray and bent and slow with age, like me
Felt the rising heat as I did then, watching
Edward and Sally sniffle slowly cheek to cheek,
Until finally, the Kool-Aide and candled cake arrived
And we all sang wide-eyed and relieved
With a new awakening of ourselves and life,
To a Sally we had never known before.

School Lunch

One slice of Big Bologna between
Two slices of pure white Wonder Bread
Four sandwiches wrapped in waxed paper
Stacked inside a brown paper bag with
Mom's cookies and a red apple for dessert.

We ate at tables separate from the hot lunchers
With their trays and no say as to the daily menu
Pitying those fellow high school students
Not valued or loved by their parents enough
To allow them to carry cold lunches

Roger who hunted, and was bologna deprived
Swapped now and then for variety when
He brought pheasant sandwiches in fall
Or venison in winter with Mayo on Wonder Bread
Cautious not to crunch the tiny beads of steel shot

Stripped of its crust, one slice of Wonder Bread
Could be rolled and compressed into a dense, yeasty ball
The size of a shooter marble and chewed slowly
Or surreptitiously tossed at one of the girls
We had known since kindergarten two tables away

We chatted and laughed with mouths full
Stupid adolescent jokes about sex
As alien as croissants or caviar
Until the bell range three times
We parted for English or Algebra class

You can find Wonder 100% Whole Wheat now
Sharing space with gluten-free and low-carb
On the eye-level supermarket shelves-
Even the multicolored bubbles on the wrapper have turned brown

Dr. Richard Allen Anderson

Dr. Richard Allen Anderson is a charter member of the Carrollton Writers Guild and of the Just Poetry group of poets. He has read his poems at every performance since the inception of the Local Voices program.

Richard took up writing as a hobby after retiring in1995 as a Senior Research Fellow from a career in Industrial Research and Development. His nine published books include four of Poetry, three books of Fiction, and two of Creative Nonfiction.

Cecilia Castro Lee

Ponderings (For my children and grandchildren)

No need to hurry, work at your own pace,
accomplish your task and be proud of yourselves.
No need to sparkle, humility brings much satisfaction.
Value your efforts and celebrate.

No need to be anyone but yourselves.
Let the light within you guide your day.
Explore, dream, discover, the path to success.
Have a heart that never hardens,
and a touch that never hurts.

Love your neighbor and love yourselves.
Fill your souls with peace and grace.

Traveling Light

Climbing a rocky mountain, step by step,
Burdened with my heavy backpack,
I plead for a helping hand.
But I'm alone on this journey.
An errant soul, striding along.

I reach the rugged top, the climax of my quest.
Catching my breath, I begin to unload
handfuls of sorrows, plenty of trials and distress,
pounds of fears, sadness and heartaches.
I cast them to the wind, *adieu*.
A leap of faith.
A flock of black birds cut across the sky.

Downhill, I travel light,
My backpack, full of hope.

Carey's Sunday Morning Nap

Sitting comfortably in his armchair
Under his favorite quilt
He dozed off into a deep sleep
Soon his snores, long and loud,
Filled the space with deafening sounds
Like a starving bear in the forest
Like a roaring lion in the desert
Like a whale upon the seas
His snoring, longer and louder, persists.

What is he dreaming about?
An adventure as a boy, running, hunting, fishing,
Plunging into an enraged creek?
Is he tackling furious foes in his football rivalry?
Is he steering his army tank through the fields of Germany?
Is he climbing the volcanos of Colombia or Machu Picchu in Peru?
Is he crossing the Amazon amid piranhas and eels?
Is he fighting traffic in the streets of Rome, Buenos Aires or Madrid?
Is he exploring Arizona, Utah or Hawaii obsessed with geography?
Is he traveling back through history to reach the painful past?
Is he struggling with his insurance or his income tax?
Or is he taking care of his dear students with so many special needs?
Maybe he's chasing his little granddaughters, his precious butterflies,
Running around the trees?

Then a moment of peace and quiet.
He opens one eye, stares at me
and asks: What time is it?

Love Overflowing

Love nestles in our hearts, a vivid emotion,
enflamed by a caress, a gentle word, a kiss.
No matter our age, young or old,
love nourishes us and builds up strength.
We must keep the sparkle alive, let it burst,
A glowing flame, a glorious moment.
Love overflowing.

Come In

Do come in.
My door is open.
There is no need to knock.
Do come in. I'm eager to see you.

The table is set
with white tablecloths and red roses.
I will sit by your side
and bask in your presence.

Like Martha,
I tend to the household.
Like Mary, my deepest yearning
is to hear your voice.

Do come in, fill my house
with your divine light.
Spread your fragrance.
Touch my soul.
Oh, Lord.

Dr. Cecilia Castro Lee

Cecilia Castro Lee is a writer, bilingual poet, literary critic, and translator. She holds a Doctoral Degree from Emory University. She is Professor Emerita from The University of West Georgia.

In 2003 she received the "Professor of the Year Award" from the Georgia Association of Teachers of Spanish and Portuguese. She has published numerous books.

She is the author of two bilingual Poetry books. *The Party is not over/ La fiesta no ha terminado* and *Words that Breathe /Palabras que respiran*. For this book, she was finalist for the Georgia Author of the Year Award (GAYA 2023).

Jessica Munn

Connection

I am here and
What was inside the sun
Grows in the leaves

What was inside the leaves
Permeates the soil

What was inside the soil
Traveled to the water

What was inside the water
Made a home in your cells

Yous lungs continuously
Made a pact with the trees
A silent exchange

Your heart keeps a steady rhythm
Drumming out your divine moments

Your emotions pass over you
Like clouds moving
Through a vast expanse

Your eyes see a doe
Licking her fawn clean
And your brain notices a kinship

Your spirit weaves connections
As though you are braiding sacred sweetgrass
Fingers passing one blade
Over another
   Over another
      Over another

Repeating
I am here
   I am here
      I am here

Graham

The flutter of you in my womb
Was like sunlight glistening
On the soft ripples of water

I gave you the name Graham
Reminiscent of golden honey
Made from bright yellow bees

On the summer day you were born
The sun ferociously roared
93 million miles away
Its beam softening
As they illuminated your flaxen hair
In a gleaming crown of light

Now a young man
I ask you to describe yourself
You look to the sky and say
"I naturally do the right thing."
Pride wells inside me
Knowing you have
No darkness to snuff out
Just an inner fire to stoke

Your essence is a soft warmth
Sharing comfort with those in need
Another boy sits
On bleachers alone
Yet you see a spotlight on him
That others have overlooked

Your small hands strike
Flint against steel
"Look Mama, I made fire"
Then you notice the breeze
Look to the trees and carefully contain it

Where will your incandescence take you?
Across mountains draped in sunlight?
Past rainbow shimmering
On the surface of the sea?
To the Northern Lights
Painting the sky in brilliance?

One day you will travel on
Your headlamp carving out the way
But if you find yourself
Dimming and listless
Feel shuffling down a dirt road
Know that back home
A porch light stays on for you

Jessica Munn

Jessica Munn is a new member of the Just Poetry group who always has a Mary Oliver book with her. She is an avid reader and appreciator of poetry, but a relatively new writer.

Jessica is grateful to the fellow members of the Carrollton Writer's Guild, whose wisdom and experience she hopes to absorb by association.

Cliff Perkins

A Poem's Power

A poem should, if it be good
Do more than entertain
The greatest seek to quietly speak
Prayers for we insane

They drag us down from solid ground
Our senses overwhelm
Set adrift in leaky ships
With no one at the helm

They storm our gates, reverberate
Confound us and confuse
Rip us apart, open our heart
'til nothing's left to lose

They steal away ordinary day
Drown us in darkest nights
Tempt us thrice with Satan's dice
Then fling us from his heights

They make us dare to float on air
Then drop us when we fall
Their blades of steel force us to feel
Tear down our every wall

They scorn our pride, know where we hide
Entomb us in their storm
Strip away all the parts we play
Strand us far from home

When all is done, we lie alone
Too weak to make a move
Washed in the blood of some bard's word
Descending like a dove

Cliff Perkins

Cliff Perkins joined the Just Poetry group in 2012. He loves reading, writing, and listening to poetry because it offers a different language – a way to say more with less – to express thoughts and feelings better and more powerfully.

Dave Rozek

Wolf

A moon midnight bright
Padded footfalls on silken, silver-white
Clouded breath of winters' chill
A flicker, a tremor, a bird's trill
Tree bark white, gray and blue
in the moon's mono chromatic frosty hue
A gray white watcher from afar
stealthily wanders near and far
On padded footfalls in the midnight bright

Lazy Kat Blu

Two fingers of scotch
Smoke swirls catchin' the flashin' neon
Lady, showin' too much leg
And a smile
her eyes a flashin'
Too hot for you, babe
Half-light, half dark,
Hides the lies
Juke blowin' the blues
Another two fingers of scotch
Another life swirls around
Chasin' the ice
Door opens and the night creeps in
Cold rain, street light yellow
Another two, stumble in
To swallow lost dreams
Cig Smoke stands on end
Till the fan blows it through
Drop a bill on the bar
For the company
Snug up the fedora, turn up the collar
Trespass into the night
Chase the wolf at the door
Till mornin' come

My Baby's Gone Blu

Sax a wailin'
Horn a blowin'
Bass a throbbin'
Drums a beatin'
Drippin' out of the club
Rainy New York streets
Soho Blue
24 hour diner
Hopper lonely
Smoke swirlin'
From my cig
Swig of
Ol' Grand Dad
New York Times
Torn up, wind blown
Chasin' pigeons
Shown up, Torn down
Ripped apart
Down and blue
Night time Park bench lonely
I sit waitin' for my boat to come in
Hopin' she'll be on it

Eagle

Flight!
Wind!
Sky!

To the precipice...
Boundless Horizons
Head of Brown, Soon to be white
Eyes, sharp, wise for such youth
With imprinted knowledge
Take to the emptiness
Open your heart, spread your soul, push out your wings!

Dave Rozek

Dave Rozek retired from a 45-year career as a broadcast radio engineer. Born in Warsaw, Poland, Dave emigrated to the United States with his adopted father.

Dave writes both sci-fi/fantasy and poetry. Many of his poems involve nature and his spirit animal, the wolf.

Gil Royal

That Kind of Friend

I want to be someone you're glad to find
On the other end when your phone rings.
Someone who brings happy thoughts to mind,
A frequent image when your spirit sings.
But more than that, someone you can trust
To be authentic, always have your back,
To even kick your backside if I must
For your own good, to get you back on track.
And when you're in a mess and need an ear,
Be someone you can pour your heart out to
And know for certain everything I hear
Will be kept secret every time you do.
That's the kind of friend I want to be
For you have been that kind of friend to me.

Beside the Shore

I know the time is coming. You will leave,
And words cannot express the way I'll feel
When you have gone, and I am here to grieve
Alone, and tend a heart that will not heal.
If ever again a happy thought should grow
And blossom unexpectedly for me,
Within my heart of broken hearts I know
Inside the seed would your reflection be.
With you I learned to ride life's bounding main,
Appreciate the ebb and flow, the tide.
Things come and go and some return again;
But you won't, having reached the other side.
Wait by the shore; you'll hear each wave renew
My promise, love, that I will come to you.

Your Inviting Eyes

I love the satin softness of your kiss,
The way you part your lips to welcome mine,
And how you show you're wanting more than this
By shifting so your curves and mine align.
That subtle movement whispers your desire
Communicates in ways words never could
To swiftly lift me from the marshy mire
Of stresses that distress more than they should.
Amazing how a simple 'need you' look
Can heal the wounded ego of a man.
No one has ever nurtured every nook
And cranny of my heart the way you can.
I give the race my all yet lose the prize,
Then all is found in your inviting eyes.

Cherish is the Word

We've shared a bed for over 50 years
And said "I love you" in so many ways.
Two hearts conjoined by sacred vows (and tears)
With memories that brighten gloomy days.
I cherish every moment that we've spent
(I was your sweet tea, you're my cognac!)
But can't recite exactly where we went
Nor resurrect details of getting back.

May not remember everything I heard,
In time forget the trail your tears have traced,
Perhaps I won't recall a single word.
The mind sometimes forgets where things are placed,
But not the heart, where all my feelings lie
Forever fresh. On that you can rely.

Gil Royal

Gil is a retired engineer whose poems have appeared in several issues of West Georgia Woman magazine. He was a regular guest on the late Nelle Reagan's radio program, "Talk of the Town," on WRGA in Rome, GA.

Robert C. Covel
Swan Song

A sudden April rain—
We dash, drenched and laughing,
Into a coffee shop.
Steaming cups of cappuccino
Make froth mustaches on our lips.
As we bet kisses on the race
Of raindrops

Coursing

Down
Window glass,
We read each other poetry—
Dickinson and Frost—
And write haiku and limericks
On notebook paper,
Which we shape into origami forms—
Yours in pristine Swan Lake forms,
Mine bedraggled Pegasus.

The clouds chase toward the horizon
As thunder tumbles of into the distance.
We emerge into the crystal air
And launch our verses
Among the rain-plucked petals
To float on serendipitous stream
From the impromptu rain.
The folded figures pirouette
Through pollen clouds
(spent seed of languid flowers),
The gold dust double gilt
By Midas touch

Of the returning sun.

Petals, pollen, and origami shapes
Swirl toward the grinning maw
Of the sewer grate
As folded wings and necks dip
In watery defeat.
They hesitate, peering into the dark,
Before the democratic flood
Sweeps all into its Stygian depths.
We shrug and smile
At temporality,
Then stroll up the petal-littered sidewalk
Beneath the dripping trees

Impermanence

The wind blows
The river flows
The butterfly knows

Life comes and goes.

Knowing Where Your Shoes Are

Your tennis shoes, tongues lolling,
Sprawl on the floor.
Black patent pumps, heels primly together,
Know their place in the closet:
Beside dress boots, self-assured
In sophisticated ease.
Your slippers snuggle beneath the bed,
Peeping from under the comforter.
Knowing where your shoes are:
Knowing you in all your moves and moods,
All the ways you walk the earth
(striding, dancing, lingering:
Knowing all the easy intimacies
That are the soul of love.

Dr. Bob Covel

Dr Covel is a retired English teacher. He has published three books of poetry and a novel, and he has another novel and another book of poetry which will be published this year. He also writes the book reviews for West Georgia Living magazine.

Anne Halliwell

Sacred Places In and Out

Sacred Places In and Out
I walk in the woods …breathing in the smell of
green and brown, the fragrance of new life
and life decomposing … ah…
ode de compost …the smell of moist earth
with the movement of worms.
I see the colors, the many shades of green
from chartreuse to the dark, ivy pine needle green.
If I turn my head fast … it is like a kaleidoscope of green
shapes, turning, dancing, blurring reality.
In this rotating green stained-glass window
I reach into my own reality. I am drawn into myself
but also beyond myself, following that tunnel
Into the shamanic underworld of myself.
Searching for me … in the new life that I am imagining.
The old me composting, and making new fresh soil
To grow the …Anne…
I could be!!!!

The New Year

We all look forward to the new year
New beginnings… another chance at getting
What we want
Creating a good life.
We can leave our failures behind
We can look at life
With a new slant….
And then create the new

Instead of making more money
Or moving up in your company
You could plant a garden
Or help a neighbor

We could give love to everyone
And love ourselves, as well
The world would improve
Love always makes the soup taste better

With our new "life song" we could
Feed all the beings …educate the masses.
Help everyone
Create a new world!!!

Why I Go to Waffle House

It used to be the only restaurant
That had cheap prices for food
It was a treat to go
And get eggs or a patty melt
They always welcome you… personally
When you come through the door
And they said goodbye when you left
Like they really cared.

Men do the cooking at the grill
Women take the orders from the tables
They shout out the orders
How do the cooks remember all the orders????

I always get the patty melt with hash browns
It comes with pickles and mayonnaise packets
The hash browns are crispy on the outside
And warn and tasty on the inside

The guests make regular visits to the Waffle House
Eating breakfast or lunch most days
Ordering the same thing everyday
The server asks ... you having your usual? ... yea

I kind of picture the waffle house as a small country church
Not white but yellow and red with a spire
All those attending saying the same thing the servers say
Good morning …How are you this morning …You doing all right?

With a Waffle House church…Our world would be a better place
War would be a bad memory
No banishing of groups
Camaraderie to the max and hash browns on the side

Anne Halliwell

Anne never liked poetry growing up. When she was in school, poetry was never a priority. She was into music. When she turned 50, she had a major change in direction and started writing poetry. She was surprised, as it was like a real poet had just stepped into her body. She guesses that would be material for her next poem.

Marc LaFountain

Butterfly

I put my face where
a yellow swallowtail lights,

it too a flower
in that verdant bush amidst
those delicious dusty colors
on its delicate, weightless body
lilting on its antelope ballerina legs.

You cannot touch a butterfly,

that's beyond possible,
beyond touch, where your
otherwise nimble, dexterous fingers
are blunt and dumb,
insensitive,
useless.

You can touch them only
when your eyes have wings
that let you land silent as
dust on down,

touch them only when
your own fluttering body's
mysterious colors
hover in the air,
subtly entangled,
already mingled with theirs

before you ever knew
those colors that light
on a flower
on a shrub,
on a face.

Oh no, unless you know how
you cannot touch a butterfly.

i earth air

i, vertical energy,
one letter spells my name

often confused
with the body's ensemble
of routes in the world

i arrive later
having been preceded
by them, implied by them,

a vertical needle
i stitch together
earth and air

i, a needle
a haystack

plants and i

we look to the sky,
plants and i,
our faces greet the rain

they summon me
i become sustenance
figuring what they need

i welcome them with a
magic touch mysteriously
working through me,
giving them space in which to spring

i am their servant,
they my ambrosia, my oracle,
we are sides of an ancient synapse

my green thumb listens to their whispers
divines their joy, their distress,
sensing when things are not right
when they are not thriving

i tend to their wounds
mending their broken stems
with small wooden splints tethered
with thin wires from straw bales

i hear them when they whimper and cry,
suffering when i know they are fading,
falling down, caught on a reverse vector
from which there is no return

at least, for some, until their reincarnation
in the alchemical hum and glow
of the forever composting earth

their radiance vibrates in me,
in its pulsing, surging forth
i become elemental verbs
that say their energy

energy that sprouts me
from some ancestral code
flowing from the earth
anchoring in the air

among them no longer am
i only animal,
more now, renewed,
revived by their presence

reaching into the sky
plants and i
shepherd, oracle

Falling Leaves

Every autumn,
like moths to a fire,
they become a great migration,
making their way to a promised land
where the remains of those before them
have already vanished, or joined some other exodus

First the daring kamikaze divers,
their weighty stems driving them down,
others a slow ferry on the river Styx
motionless save their downward flow,
some dervishes spinning funnels of dizzy spirals,
others frenzied, ecstatic in their squirrelly orbits

Then the nonchalant and lackadaisical,
perhaps procrastinators looking forward
to putting off the inevitable,
the reckless lamenting no chance
of doing the same

Acrobats tumbling, twirling,
none in pairs, just ensembles of solitaires,
random, haphazard, a slow relentless
blizzard of players doing their part disappearing
before the darkness of the coming solstice

Gliding sideways, the shifty hope to defy gravity,
rising upward, others seek to reverse
its spell, returning to the mother
hovering above who seems
to have forsaken them

Many meander aimlessly,
oblivious to their destiny,
making believe they are not yet dead

Mercurial comedians bring humor
but we don't know why they're funny,
insufferably aloof ballerinas move
with indifferent confidence,
dramatic flamencos feverishly
wallow in the anguish of falling

Under a slate sky they are still now,
like a blanket of snow silently
dappling the woods' floor with
blanched shades of ochre, sienna, umber,
peering up at those who have not yet
made the leap or have not yet lost their grip

Dr. Marc LaFountain

Marc LaFountain, born in Massachusetts, grew up on the east end of Long Island. After receiving his PhD in Sociology from the University of Tennessee, he taught at several universities before joining the University of West Georgia in 1977. He retired from there in 2008.

He is the author of *Dali and Postmodernism: This is Not an Essence* (SUNY Press, 1997). His book of poems, *Left Wanting More*, was published by Vabella Press, 2015. A second collection of poems, *Solar Winds*, was published by Dancing Crows Press, 2021.

Alan Caldwell

Titanium

I let my dog lap the last few drops of coffee
in my "Greatest Husband" cup
I'm not sure coffee is good for a dog
or for a man for that matter
accounts vary

I'm also not sure I'm the greatest husband
or even the goodest one
or even a mediocre one
accounts vary there as well

coffee cups are not responsible for the lies
or exaggerations
disseminated on their behalf
I once threw my wedding band
into a campfire
a shameful account she's never heard
and maybe nothing to write a poem about

I almost lied to you
and claimed that I don't know why I did it
that shameful act

I feign ignorance a lot
but I can't pull that here
not this time

I did it because
it was an almost-endless dismal winter
because I don't know how to be a husband
or a father
or maybe even a man
because I had no models to emulate

and no maps to follow
because I believed
and maybe still believe
that happiness isn't for me
or for us
all of us who are afraid of the dark
all of us who can't tolerate the itch of our collars
on the backs of our necks
all of us who smell funeral flowers
long after the graves are filled
and the other mourners are safe at home

the next morning I dug through the still-warm coals
with the old Case knife my daddy gave me

I found the ring
smoked
but safe

titanium melts at thirty-five hundred degrees
maybe my fire was somewhat less than that
or maybe my fire harbored a cooler spot
some sheltered recess to cloister
a mediocre husband's foolishness

Variety

he'd say daddy
can I have a snack plate for breakfast?
a vy-are-uh-tee
he'd say
you know what I mean daddy

he couldn't pronounce variety

he liked cantaloupe
and cheddar cheese
and buttered toast
and maple bacon

a vy-are-uh-tee
he'd say
you know what I mean daddy

it was just the two of us back then
June and July and August
I was a teacher
as if a teacher
could ever be anything else
but a teacher
as if a father
could ever be anything else
but a father

after breakfast
I'd drive my old green truck
to the industrial park
get out our chairs
my big chair
his tiny chair

we'd sit and wait
beneath the last rebellious pine
a loblolly or maybe it was a slash
or a short-leaf
I can't recall

trains passed about every
quarter hour or so
the drivers
or the engineers
would wave
and blow their lonesome whistle

and blow their lonesome whistle

when we got back home
when it was warmer
we'd go for a swim
in our little pool
I'd throw him in
again
and again
and again
till he was tired
and hungry

he'd say daddy
can I have a snack plate for lunch?
a vy-are-uh-tee
he'd say
you know what I mean daddy

he couldn't pronounce variety

I called him last night
one father to another
as if a father
could ever be anything else
but a father

he was making the baby a snack plate
a variety
he said
just a variety

Alan Caldwell

Alan Caldwell is a recently-retired teacher, a husband, a father, a grandfather, and, most recently, a writer. In only two years, his work has been featured more than fifty times in literary journals and magazines. Two of his short stories have been nominated for the Pushcart Prize. In May of 2024, Close To the Bone Publishing released a compilation of his short stories, *However Small and Hidden*, to rave reviews and modest sales. His first collection of poetry, *The Only Verse,* was published April 2025.

Carol Abney

Almon Street
(written in honor of those
who have lost loved ones)

When I moved in,
Unsure and directionless,
You asked me to love you
And to take care of you
As if you were shiny and new,
    Just like we all do.

And I spent each day in gratitude
For your shelter from the cascade of rain,
For a place to sleep at night
Peaceful and unencumbered,
Listening to the silence of your rooms,
Your roof like a soaring cathedral,
Your foundation, strong as a stone mason,
    Just as we all are.

And now that I must leave you,
You, who have held me close,
Encompassed me, and helped lift my gaze upwards
For six long years,
The tears cascade in waterfalls,

For I have healed here, and I have
Watched my son grow into a principled man
Of honor and driving purpose,
And I have learned new things -
Siding repair, how to caulk, paint, clean gutters, and
Beautify, how to use a reel mower, create a garden,
And how to help others, thus finding my own purpose
In a seemingly directionless world,
> *Just as we all must.*

And on this day, as the rain
Slowly dissipates, gently pattering
Against your metal roof,
The sun starts to shine again,
Softly filtered golden rays
Stretching from heaven to earth,
And a rainbow forms across the still-gray sky.

With a certainty borne of walking through
Upheaval unscathed and the aching necessity
Of moving out of my comfort zone,
I know that, as I move away,
You will open your doors to another family,
And they will find a peaceful home in you,
And they will find laughter, and
New beginnings, and transportive strength
To overcome heartache,
> *Just as I have done.*

The Gift

(The wonderful joy of receiving forgiveness and release from the prison of guilt)

Imagine
That you are going fishing,
And you have a big bucket of worms,
Alive and wriggling in the soft soil and compost.

The bucket is full, and the worms are slimy,
Creepy, crawly - the best bait ever.

That's what my mistakes are like -
A big bucket filled with muck,
Bait for every bad boyfriend, fraud,
Crooked repairman, and general bad actor,
Saying
Look, here I am, ready for you to
Hook onto – come join me in a downward-spiraling
Synthesis of despair.

And in the midst of this worm-filled life,
As I struggle mightily to lift myself
Out of the dark, stagnant water, and
Up onto the bank of the rumbling river
Where the fresh breeze causes
The leaves of trees to lilt and sway,
And the melody of cricket, frog, and bird songs
Intertwine to form
A harmonious sunshine symphony,

I see a far-away, grassy meadow,
And I run to it,
Lie down in it, and make grass angels,
And laugh,
And you are there, and
You give me a gift.

I earnestly ask for your forgiveness
And you say in reply,
There was nothing ever to forgive.
But my big bucket of a million mistakes,
I stammer out,
And you say,
It's okay.
You are human.

And the unexpected, undeserved gift
Of your compassion
Resonates through my life even now,
A constant song like the bird-voiced treefrog
In the wooded swamp near the river,
Giving me strength to set the worms free,

And to fill my bucket
instead
With holy water,
With blossoming flowers.

Age is Just a Number

Being young was wild and fun -
I would play and play all day,
Chasing the sun 'round a big green field,
Trying to catch a ray.

Laughing until my stomach hurt
At the jokes and stories of my friends,
Enjoying popsicles, checkers, Frisbee, and games,
Wishing the day would never end.
I heard my mother calling
As bright stars shimmered in the sky.
Time for macaroni and cheese, please,
And I sadly waved goodbye.

Age is just a number,
I've heard many wise men say,
So still I run,
Catching luminescent sun rays,

Glad for the age
I am today.

Carol Abney

Carol Abney published her first book of poetry, *A Chorus of Hope*, in 2024. Carol is a retired high school English teacher who received Teacher of the Year honors three times.

She appreciates the power of poetry to provide hope, healing, humor, and observations about the world around us.

LOCAL VOICES

INDEX

Anderson, Richard Allen	8-10
Biography	11
First Day	8
Sally's Birthday	9
School Lunch	10
Abney, Carol	6, 52-56
Biography	57
Age is Just a Number	56
Almon Street	52
The Gift	54
Caldwell, Alan	2, 46-48
Biography	51
Lovely Face (For Eleanor)	2
Titanium	46
Variety	48
Covel, Robert C.	1, 31-33
Biography	34
Gone (For Eleanor)	1
Impermanence	32
Knowing Where Your Shoes Are	33
Swan Song	31
Halliwell, Anne	4, 35-37
Biography	38
Ode to a Poet	4
Sacred Places In and Out	35
The New Year	36
Why I Go to Waffle House	37
LaFountain, Marc	39-43
Biography	45
Butterfly	39
Falling Leaves	43
i earth air	40
plants and i	41
Lee, Cecilia Castro	3, 12-15
Biography	16
Carey's Sunday Morning Nap	14
Come In	15
Love Overflowing	15
On Being Human (Missing Eleanor)	3
Ponderings	12
Traveling Light	13

Munn, Jessica	5, 17-18
Biography	19
Connection	17
For Eleanor	5
Graham	18
Perkins, Cliff	20
Biography	21
A Poem's Power	20
Royal, Gil	26-29
Biography	30
Beside the Shore	27
Cherish is the Word	29
That Kind of Friend	26
Your Inviting Eyes	29
Rozek, Dave	22-25
Biography	25
Eagle	25
Lazy Kat Blu	23
My Baby's Gone Blu	24
Wolf	22

The Carrollton Writers Guild is a nonprofit organization dedicated to encouraging the literary arts. Participation is open to adults writing fiction/nonfiction, memoirs, and poetry. It is a supportive environment providing skill enhancement and critique. For more information, visit carrolltonwritersguild.org.

Carrollton Writers Guild
PO Box 2193
Carrollton, GA 30112

www.ingramcontent.com/pod-product-compliance
Lightning Source LLC
Chambersburg PA
CBHW061805070526
44586CB00023B/2716